D1174205

The Ten Golden Rules

The Ten Golden Rules

Ancient Wisdom from the Greek Philosophers on Living the Good Life

M. A. Soupios, PhD
and
Panos Mourdoukoutas, PhD

HAMPTON ROADS
PUBLISHING COMPANY, INC.

Cover design by Michele Weatherbee

Hampton Roads Publishing Company, Inc.
1125 Stoney Ridge Road
Charlottesville, VA 22902

434-296-2772
fax: 434-296-5096
e-mail: hrpc@hrpub.com
www.hrpub.com

If you are unable to order this book from your local bookseller, you may order directly from the publisher.
Call 1-800-766-8009, toll-free.

Library of Congress Cataloging-in-Publication Data

Soupios, Michael A., 1949-
[Ten rules of spiritual and professional fulfillment]
The ten golden rules : ancient wisdom from the Greek philosophers on living the good life / Michael Soupios and Panos Mourdoukoutas.
p. cm.
Originally published: The ten rules of spiritual and professional fulfillment. Greece : Klidarithmos, 2006.
Summary: "How the wisdom of ancient Greek philosophers can be applied to modern problems and concerns to create a more spiritual existence"—Provided by publisher.
ISBN 978-1-57174-605-4 (alk. paper)
1. Conduct of life. 2. Philosophy, Ancient. I. Mourdoukoutas, Panos. II. Title.
BJ1581.2.S638 2009
170'.44—dc22

2008050591

ISBN 978-1-57174-605-4
10 9 8 7 6 5 4 3 2 1
Printed on acid-free paper in the United States

To ancient Greeks,
the giants of Philosophy

Contents

Preface

In our culture the pursuit of the good life, that is, a life rich with opportunity for human development, has become a near universal ideal, but it is hardly of recent origin. For the vast majority of history, human aspiration extended no further than the necessities of food, clothing, and shelter—a situation in which the notion of "higher" needs was simply inconceivable. Today, thanks to the blessings of science, industry, and technology, the material obstacles that once precluded human fulfillment have been overcome, and significant numbers of people are now becoming aware of a paradox, namely, an inverse correlation between material prosperity and spiritual contentment: economic well-being is not in itself a guarantee of the fuller satisfactions instinctively sought. A life filled with trendy restaurants and designer labels may, in the short term, amuse and exhilarate, but in the end it leaves people highly dissatisfied and yearning for something decidedly more spiritual. Modernity faces a daunting and unprecedented challenge—to somehow remain a culture of plenty while simultaneously addressing the needs of the inner life. Only if this incongruent challenge is successfully met can a life worth living be attained.

For centuries, most discussions of spirituality in Western culture have concentrated on the precepts and practices of the Judeo-Christian tradition. For more than two thousand years, any consideration of the spiritual life fell within the privileged domain of organized religion. But the rise of modern secularism in the eighteenth and nineteenth centuries severely compromised the credibility of the religious path, raising a serious dilemma for the modern West—the spiritual imperatives of life continue to demand our attention at a time when traditional mechanisms for addressing these needs have become increasingly dysfunctional and ineffective.

A potential source of remedy for this situation lies in an appeal to a distinctively different tradition, one that does not rely upon faith but instead seeks to arrive at spiritual insight by the alternative route of rational inquiry. This approach constitutes the core legacy of ancient Hellenism, the gift bestowed upon Western civilization by the likes of Socrates, Plato, Aristotle, Epictetus, Epicurus, and others. Unlike the God-centered perspectives of the Hebrews, the ancient Greeks made humanity the focus of their cultural enterprise. In *Antigone,* Sophocles epitomized Greek attitudes in this regard when he described man as the most "wondrous" of creatures. Above all, the quality that distinguished humanity, the essence that endowed our species with its wondrous potentials, was reason, man's rational capacity that allowed humanity to live in harmony with the order of Being and ensured our capacity for a life-code independent of divine mandate. Reason can confer its own unique spiritual discernments, even in the absence of miter and chalice.

The ten rules that follow represent enduring features of the Greek wisdom. In a very real sense, they defy time and place and represent insights that remain profoundly relevant for contemporary culture. They can serve as antidotes for an age in which much that is true and valuable has been obscured by falsity and misconception. Accordingly, these ancient aphorisms are offered to all those interested in rubbing the dust from their eyes.

INTRODUCTION
FAITH AND REASON

In its many varieties and forms, spiritual living has for centuries been the special province of faith as opposed to reason. Religious preachers of all sorts set their own rules and procedures for peace of mind and salvation. Without question, religious institutions have played a powerful role in expanding the spiritual horizon of humanity. At the same time, however, the varying religious prescriptions have given rise to violent factionalism. Rather than serving as a source of common spiritual insight, the different theologies have too often resulted in blood and mayhem. Religious conviction without consideration of rational potentials has often proved an obstacle to scientific and economic progress and, eventually, to the spiritual state of humanity.

In this book we argue that the gifts of a spiritual existence can be attained by other means, by means more universal than culturally determined particularities of religious belief, namely, reason. Notwithstanding the many accidents of birth (race, ethnicity, cultural setting, etc.), all men and women ultimately share a common unifying core in the form of a rational capacity. Above all, it is this endowment that constitutes our universal essence as human beings and it is this same endowment that presents opportunity for spiritual insight. In great measure these are the premises attributed to the great philosophical sages of ancient Greece. Intellectuals such as Plato, Aristotle, Epicurus, and Epictetus provided their own form of spiritual understanding without the agitations and instabilities of religious devotion. Plato, for instance, argues that human fulfillment requires an examined life and that virtue is always rewarded in some sense. Epictetus and the Stoics spoke of *apatheia* (apathy) and *adiaphora* (indifference), the ideal states of mind of truly wise persons, individuals who systematically discount the many distresses that life sends their way. Only the positive experiences are allowed to gain entry to this citadel. The rest are denied admission by the most powerful of gatekeepers—reason. Aristotle tells us to forge true friendships that are nurtured and treasured in relations imbued with trust and amity. Epicurus tells us to avoid shallow and transient pleasures. Keep your life simple. Seek calming joys that contribute to peace of mind. True pleasure is disciplined and restrained. Pythagoras tells us to be responsible human beings, to reproach ourselves with honesty and thoughtfulness for wrongdoing; to assume responsibility for our own errors; and to be prepared to accept the consequences. Aeschylus advises us not to be prosperous fools. Hesiod tells us not to do evil to others because in the end we do evil to ourselves, while Aesop speaks to us of the rewards of human kindness.

In the chapters that follow, the ancient wisdom of spiritual living by reason is codified in ten simple rules:

Rule 1: Examine Life

Rule 2: Worry Only about the Things You Can Control

Rule 3: Treasure Friendship

Rule 4: Experience True Pleasure

Rule 5: Master Yourself

Rule 1

Examine Life

The unexamined life is not worth living.
—Plato

Rule 1
Examine Life

When a 103-year-old man living in the mountains of Messinia—at the tip of mainland Greece—was asked what his secret was, his answer was fairly simple: "I have always kept myself busy. I have been living my life. My hair has turned white, my hands and feet are not as strong as they used to be, but I can still reason. And as long as I reason, as long as I keep my mind engaged, my spirit, my soul is at peace. I can still examine and experience the world around me and participate in it, that's what makes me happy. I can reason under the pine tree how to make better baskets. It now takes longer—much longer than it used to take to make each one of them. But it doesn't matter. I no longer make them to earn a living. I make them just for the beauty of it, just for the pleasant thought of young men carrying grapes in vineyards. I can still examine life in the village coffee shop, where I debate local, national, and international issues with my fellow villagers and meet new people visiting the area. I examine life in the village church, where I raise anew the question of our being. I examine life on the farm, where I still plant and nurture olive trees, dreaming of the days the new generation will harvest them, and cut branches to crown Olympic victors. I examine life by my fireplace. I . . . ," the old man went on and on. "The day I stop examining life, I will be dead." *That was two years later, just three months shy of his 105th birthday.*

This old man's message about life states loudly and clearly the first rule of spiritual living by reason:

Examine life, engage life with a vengeance; always search for new pleasures and new destinies to reach with your mind.

This rule isn't new. It echoes the thought of ancient Greek philosophers and most notably that of Plato through the voice of his hero, Socrates. Living life is about examining life through reason, nature's greatest gift to humanity. The importance of reason in sensing and examining life is evident in all phases of life—from the infant who strains to explore its new surroundings to the grandparent who actively reads and assesses the headlines of the daily paper. Reason lets human beings participate in life. To be human is to think, appraise, and explore the world, discovering new sources of material and spiritual pleasure.

Some people fully understand the significance of reason in examining and participating in life. They espouse new ideas, long for new things and new relationships; they are constantly discovering new interests, escaping from their boring routines. They engage life with enthusiasm, grasping life aggressively and squeezing from it every drop of excitement, satisfaction, and joy. Some discover new professional challenges, build new bridges or new skyscrapers, develop new medicines or new computer gear.

Others discover new hobbies, scaling mountaintops or exploring the sea bottom or the depths of the jungle. A third group addresses the ills of humanity, the sick, the poor, and the disadvantaged, and amasses funds, food, and medicine to comfort and cure them.

A properly examined life protects people against living life as spectators. It bestows the opportunities that accompany every sunrise and it does so even for those who are no longer in their youth. People who continue to explore life fully, even though they may be advanced in years, can still discover that something new awaits them every day regardless of age—a new place to travel, a new book to read, new people to meet. The key to unleashing the potential of reason is attitude. The person who approaches life with childlike wonder is best prepared to defy the limitations of time, is more "alive," is more of a participant in life at the age of sixty or even seventy than the average teenager.

That's the case of John, who, after retiring from a sales job in his early sixties, got a university job as a student career counselor. Suddenly, his life took on new purpose and meaning. Every day, he looked forward to getting to his office and to helping young people with their careers, forgetting all about getting old or gaining extra income. Nick's story is more intriguing. After retiring in his early sixties from his financial planning job, he opened up a World Tea House in a retirement community. His life, too, found a new purpose and meaning. Every day, he looked forward to meeting his patrons, sharing a cup of tea with them, listening to their life stories, comforting them and being comforted by them. "Retiring isn't about resting on the couch or in bed. It is about doing the things you want to do. It is about working not for money, but for the pleasure of the things you accomplish." James followed a different path. After retiring in his mid-fifties from his banking job, he moved to Southern California, where he turned his stock market trading hobby and knowledge of the financial market into a new career. He became a certified financial planner and developed a large clientele who sought his knowledge and experience to manage their finances. Sometimes, James assisted his clients on a pro bono basis. Other times, he charged a small fee. Yet this new vocation was much different from the old career. He saw clients in his own place at his own pace, without a boss above him, monitoring his performance.

Unfortunately, not everyone fully understands the significance and potentialities of reason. Some people fail to cultivate and utilize it to its fullest extent, and fail therefore to participate in a fully human existence.

Life is full of potential but too often people settle for a series of stale routines, allowing themselves to become content with the dull and ordinary activities that have guided their lives for years. They abandon the sense of adventure that once colored their lives and instead accept one compromise after another, staying on the sidelines of life, isolating and alienating themselves from friends and relatives. That's the case of Ted, who, after taking advantage of an early retirement package, put an end to his thirty-year computer engineering career, sold his New York house, and moved to a retirement facility. There he settled for routine activities, such as playing golf with the same people in the same place, dining in the same places, watching the same television shows. Slowly, he lost interest in anything that took him out of these routines, anything that engaged his mind in adventurous things, such as travel or politics.

Often the source of these gray patterns is the conventional wisdom imposed on us by the society in which we live. Culture has a powerful capacity to shape our values, beliefs, and perspectives that often reflect a bias on behalf of the status quo; it does not encourage change or innovation as much as it does compliance with traditional modes and orders.

In other words, the societal setting in which we live counsels us to endorse received opinion, to accept the customary and the time-honored. The price of non-conformity in these matters can be very high. Those with the courage to challenge convention may feel a sense of disloyalty and guilt and, in particular, they can experience a pronounced sense of isolation.

Ultimately, the critical cross-examination of life advocated by Socrates must be seen as an act of courage. It represents the path less traveled and is therefore filled with uncertainty and risk. At the same time, however, the rewards awaiting those with the courage to truly examine life are great indeed because for such individuals, every day is a fresh beginning filled with prospect and possibility. Above all, what these individuals come to understand is that convictions can be prisons. They restrict the human spirit and delimit our potential for living. The richer and wider view of life we all seek is reserved for those who take their cue from Socrates—the unexamined life is not worth living.

The Meditation Grid

≈ *Approach life with childlike wonder.*

≈ *Engage life with a vengeance without preconception.*

≈ *When the mind is engaged, the soul is most alive.*

≈ *Grasp life aggressively and squeeze from it every drop of excitement, satisfaction, and joy.*

≈ *Always search for new things, new pleasures.*

≈ *Something new is always waiting for you: a place you haven't visited, a book you haven't read, a friend you haven't met, a meal you haven't tasted.*

Rule 2

Worry Only about the Things You Can Control

Remove utterly your desire; for if you desire some one of the things that are not under your control you are bound to be unfortunate. . . . Whoever, therefore, wants to be free, let him neither wish anything, nor avoid anything, that is under the control of others; or else he is necessarily a slave. . . . Never say about anything, "I have lost it," but only "I have given it back . . . It is not things themselves that disturb men, but their judgments about these things."

—Epictetus

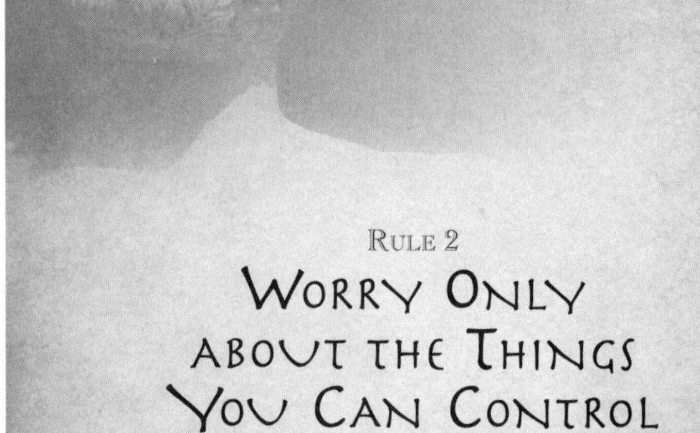

Rule 2

Worry Only about the Things You Can Control

Pamela never worried about the things under her control, the things she had a choice to pursue or not to pursue: she dropped out of college, married someone she met in a bar a few weeks earlier, and changed jobs every other month. She always worried about the things that weren't in her control: about things that happened in the past, about growing older, about the behavior of her parents, her husband, her children, and her boss. She pointed the finger at them for whatever was wrong in her life, and wasted her energies trying to change them, all to no avail. Now in her late sixties, three times divorced, Pamela lives alone, running from one therapist to another trying to find sanity in her mind and peace in her soul.

Tiffany, on the other hand, has always focused on the things under her control: she carefully planned her education and chose her husband, her friends, and her business associates. She never troubled herself with things that happened in the past, never pointed the finger at others for whatever went wrong in her life, and never wasted energy attempting to change them. Now in her early sixties, Tiffany lives with her husband, has two grown children who treasure her, and has never required the services of a therapist to work out her problems.

Pamela's and Tiffany's stories highlight the second rule of spiritual living by reason:

WORRY ONLY ABOUT THE THINGS UNDER YOUR CONTROL, THE THINGS THAT CAN BE INFLUENCED AND CHANGED BY YOUR ACTIONS, NOT ABOUT THE THINGS THAT ARE BEYOND YOUR CAPACITY TO DIRECT OR ALTER.

This rule summarizes several important features of ancient Stoic wisdom—features that remain powerfully suggestive for modern times. Most notable is the belief in an ultimately rational order operating in the universe, reflecting a benign providence that ensures proper outcomes in life. Thinkers such as Epictetus did not simply prescribe "faith" as an abstract philosophical principle; they offered concrete strategies based on intellectual and spiritual discipline. The key to resisting the hardship and discord that intrude upon every human life is to cultivate a certain attitude toward adversity based on the critical distinction between those things we are able to control versus those that are beyond our capacity to manage. Misguided investors may not be able to recover their fortunes, but they can resist the tendency to engage in self-torment. The victims of a natural disaster, major illnesses, or accidents may not be able to recover and live their lives the way they used to, but they too can save themselves the self-torment. In other words, while we cannot control all of the outcomes we seek in life, we certainly can control our responses to these outcomes. Herein lies our potential for a life that is both happy and fulfilled.

Unfortunately, no one is endowed with an unlimited supply of energy. Worrying about the things that are not in our control is wasteful and destructive. It consumes our energies, and tends to prolong and exacerbate misfortune. Understanding this simple premise of life and having the wisdom, the will, and the discipline to focus on the things we can control while steering away from the things we cannot control is the basis for allocating our energies efficiently and effectively, and for living in harmony and peace with ourselves and with our environment.

In a free society, one of the things in our control is the path of our social life, the choice between the things to pursue and the things not to pursue, a career, a business, an education, and a family. Another thing in our control is the choice of the people with whom we associate: our spouses, our friends, our business associates, our legislators. Other things in our control are the places where we want to live and work, the entertainment we seek, the clothes we wear, and the desire for things we would like to own.

One of the things not in our control, but in the control of nature, is aging, the passing through different stages in life, the change of our physical appearance and mental status. Some people age at a faster pace, while others do so at a slower rate, but we all age with the passing of time. This rule has no exceptions! Another thing that is not in our control is death, the final act of our being. Some people will die at an earlier age from accidents and illnesses, while others will die at a later age from natural causes, but one day, we will all die. This rule has no exceptions either! Nature eventually takes back what it gives. This means that we don't actually lose our lives, but that we just return to nature that which was given in the first place. A third thing not in our control is the behavior of the people surrounding us, the behavior of our spouses, our children, our friends, our business associates, our co-workers and supervisors. A fourth thing not in our control is the past, the things that have already happened, pleasant or unpleasant, that cannot be retrieved or altered.

Understanding the things that affect our lives, separating those we can command from those we can't, worrying only about the things we can control, focusing only on the problems we can solve isn't easy. It takes wisdom, will, determination, and discipline. It takes wisdom to understand the limits nature imposes on us, the different stages it presents to us, and wisdom to understand that we cannot change people and institutions we don't have control over. It takes will and determination to accept the adverse consequences of the things we don't control, the pleasant and unpleasant consequences of our aging, the unpleasant thoughts of our own death or the death of people we love, the adverse effects of the behavior of others, and the adversity of the things that happened in the past. It takes discipline to learn to shift our energies and efforts from the things we don't control to the things we do. It takes discipline to keep our minds from slipping and sliding toward the unpleasant consequences that arise from pursuing things that aren't in our control.

In some cases, people are fortunate enough to have the ability to distinguish between the things they control and those they don't, separating the one group from the other and focusing only on the group of things they do control. They can get up in the morning and raise a simple question for every problem faced: Is the solution to this problem in my grasp? If not, let me consider the next problem, and the next, until I isolate the problems I can solve.

We can, for instance, look at ourselves in the mirror and notice our hair thinning or turning white, and ask the question: Can I do anything about that? Perhaps hair transplants or coloring is the temporary but not the permanent solution to the problem. In either case, hair whitening and thinning is part of the aging process, under nature's control, not ours, and therefore, we needn't worry. On to the next problem.

I am unhappy with my job. Can I change it? Is it in my control? If yes, I will outline the steps I have to take to pursue another job. If not, if my current situation makes a job change impossible, then it doesn't help to worry. On to the next question.

In some cases, people aren't as fortunate. We believe, or want to believe, that all things are in our control and that we can change them in the direction we want. Some of us believe or want to believe that life lasts forever. We are engaged in the accumulation of assets, real estate, money, paintings, things that will appreciate in value over time and offer us a better life sometime in the future. Others believe that aging and death are but the first act of our existence, to be followed by a different life as described by some religious text. As a result, they forgo the consumption of the things that give them pleasure today in exchange for things that might give them pleasure sometime in the future.

Perhaps we believe we can change the behavior of our spouses or our children. We expect things from them they cannot deliver. Then we begin pointing the finger at them, blaming others for the things that go wrong in our lives, engaging in quarrels, wasting our energies on the things we don't control.

Others fix their mental energies on the past, on the things that have already happened and the pleasant or adverse conditions they have produced. They try to go back and erase negative experiences or relive those that had a positive effect on them. In this way, they are enslaved by the things they do not control and ignore the things that are in their control. By living in the past, they fail to live in the present, because they have little or no energy to allocate toward the available things that might make their life better.

In short, no one can realistically provide cure-alls for the emotional stresses and the traumas that life inevitably inflicts upon us. Yet the ancient Stoics have provided a rational approach to such adversities. They have successfully demonstrated that, to a very substantial degree, we are the authors of our own misery. By dwelling upon the irretrievable, we not only guarantee many sleepless nights, we also drain precious energy and focus away from the things we can remedy. Perhaps most important, we deny ourselves that sense of spiritual peace and well-being that is one of life's great blessings. Those who weep over spilled milk are condemned to a life of mopping-up. The rational alternative is to detach ourselves from the things we cannot influence and to rely upon actions that allow for fruitful living. Worrying about the things that are under our control requires wisdom, the ability to distinguish things we control from those we don't, and discipline to learn how to shift our focus from the things we can't control to the things we can.

The Meditation Grid

≈ ***Cultivate a certain attitude.***

≈ ***For every problem you face, ask a simple question.***

≈ ***Is this problem in my control?***

≈ ***If not, I forget all about it. On to the next problem.***

≈ ***If yes, what can I do about it?***

≈ ***What are my options?***

≈ ***What is the required energy?***

Rule 3
Treasure Friendship

Friendship is a relationship in which two people come to share the same soul.

—Aristotle

Rule 3
Treasure Friendship

Gloria owns a successful business. She lives in a spacious house with elegant furnishings. She drives a brand-new car, and shops at the best stores in town. But she isn't content with life. Though she knows many people, whom at one point or another she considered friends, she has yet to experience a true reciprocal relationship. She often feels lonely and depressed. Gloria's problem has become all too common in contemporary society. She has never come to the understanding that friendship is a relationship of trust, a quality, not a quantity, but has always confused friendship with friendly acquaintances and "utility relationships," counting her "friends" by the dozens.

Helen works as a secretary in a small company. She lives in a modest, simply furnished apartment. She drives an old car and shops at discount stores. But she is content with her life.

She rarely feels lonely and depressed, and she has never seen a therapist. Helen's secret is that she has two good friends who stand by her and share the laughter and tears of life. She understands that friendship is about quality, not quantity, and she has never confused "utility friendships" and friendly acquaintances with true friendship. She has invested the time and energy to nurture genuine relationships.

Gloria's and Helen's stories highlight the third rule of spiritual living by reason:

FRIENDSHIP IS A RECIPROCAL ATTACHMENT THAT FILLS THE NEED FOR AFFILIATION. FRIENDSHIP CANNOT BE ACQUIRED IN THE MARKETPLACE, BUT MUST BE NURTURED AND TREASURED IN RELATIONS IMBUED WITH TRUST AND AMITY.

According to Greek philosophy, one of the defining characteristics of humanity that distinguishes it from other forms of existence is a deeply engrained social instinct, the need for association and affiliation with others, a need for friendship. Socrates, Plato, and Aristotle viewed the formation of society as a reflection of the profound need for human affiliation rather than simply a contractual arrangement between otherwise detached individuals. Gods and animals do not have this kind of need, but for humans it is an indispensable aspect of a life worth living because one cannot speak of a completed human identity, nor of true happiness, without the associative bond called "friendship." No amount of wealth, status, or power can adequately compensate for a life devoid of genuine friends.

"True" friendship is governed by a strictly qualitative logic, that is, friendship is a rare spiritual intimacy that can only be shared among a handful of people. As a result, a person may live an entire life and only possess three or four "real" friends. Too many people assume they are blessed because they can name fifty or sixty individuals whom they designate as friends. In truth, numbers such as these indicate neither good fortune nor extraordinary popularity, but a complete misunderstanding of genuine friendship. Specifically, those who number their friendships in the dozens have confused friendly acquaintances with actual friendships. An individual cannot befriend a crowd because friendship requires a willingness to sacrifice one's own well-being for the good of the other. Such intimate devotion can be extended only within certain very narrow limits. Accordingly, real friendship is not to be understood quantitatively—by its very nature, friendship will involve a small number of high-quality relationships.

What sort of person is capable of engaging in true friendship? Despite our strong social instincts, some people will never be able to establish, much less maintain, anything approximating the bond of friendship, because friendship requires that both parties possess a certain moral stature. Friendship is, above all, a relationship of trust. For individuals morally incapable of respecting and upholding the trust placed in them by other persons, the kind of amity considered here becomes impossible. This explains why criminals of every stripe are incapable of friendships. Their relationships are always fundamentally predatory and, therefore, inconsistent with the reciprocal attachments that make for real friends. The most that can be said of the relationships established by those who are vice-prone is that they are transient affairs, driven by impure motives that ultimately render friendship inconceivable.

Friendship shouldn't be confused with pseudo-friendship, or "utility relationships" that have become commonplace these days. Many people mistakenly believe that utility relationships are acceptable illustrations of friendships, but they aren't. Utility relationships may be contractual, they may be a financial alliance, they may involve a political attachment of some sort, but none of these relationships should be confused with friendship because in every instance the association is driven by an ulterior motive. That's the case with George's friendships. As the president of a large corporation, he boasted of the many friends he had. Every other day, someone would invite him and his family to dinner. His Christmas reception list included scores of people who never turned down his invitation. Yet most of these friendships were "utility relationships," financial alliances that ended as soon as he stepped down from his position.

Financial concerns, political considerations, and the possibilities of establishing fruitful contacts are not the proper foundations for legitimate friendships. Rather, they imply a tacit exploitation in which people are in some sense "used" for the benefit of others. What these relationships typically lack despite the superficial pleasantries that often accompany them is a meaningful concern for the other person as a person—one of the indispensable features of a true friendship.

In short, friendship is a near sacred bond between individuals, a mutual nobility that requires duty, obligation, commitment, and sacrifice, a difficult and challenging standard seldom found in the majority of relationships experienced in life. Yet, when on some rare occasions we are fortunate enough to forge such a relationship, our entire life is changed. All that we experience takes on a new meaning when we are in a position to share completely with a person who has become "another self." No amount of power, money, or status can substitute for the precious joys of a true friend. As Aristotle said, friendship is a relationship in which two people come to share the same soul. In the absence of this soul-mate, life lacks energy and meaning.

THE MEDITATION GRID

≈ *Friendship is a reciprocal attachment that fills the need for affiliation.*

≈ *Wealth and power are not the basis of friendships.*

≈ *Friendship is nurtured by relations imbued with trust and amity.*

≈ *Friendship shouldn't be confused with friendly acquaintances or "utility relationships."*

≈ *Friendship can only be shared with a few people who respect and uphold the trust placed in them by others.*

≈ *Friendship must be understood qualitatively, not quantitatively.*

≈ *Without friendship life lacks energy and meaning.*

Rule 4

Experience True Pleasure

By pleasure we mean the absence of pain in the body and of turmoil in the mind.
—Epicurus

Rule 4

Experience True Pleasure

Maria has never really satisfied her wants and desires. She has always been dedicated to shallow and transient pleasures, complicating her life with too much entertainment and too much work. On weekends, she dines out at the finest restaurants in town, and runs from one night club to another, seeking the company of any man who shows her the least bit of interest. On weekdays, she works two jobs, neither of which she enjoys, but which are necessary to fund her lavish lifestyle. Lately, her sleep has been disrupted by a variety of anxious thoughts regarding the quality of her meaningless and disordered existence. She seems incapable of dismissing the trivialities that clutter her life

Pamela exudes a sense of purpose and priority. She has never been dedicated to the sorts of fads and trends that command other people's lives. Simplicity and balance are the principles that govern her affairs. Rather than wasting money on high-profile restaurants and clubs, she prefers spending time with family and a few close friends. She is involved in a solid relationship with a man she's dated for three years. They have a variety of common interests, including poetry and the theater. As an elementary school teacher, Pamela derives enormous satisfaction from helping young children reach their potential. Unlike many women her age, she has come to appreciate the virtue and necessity of periodically setting aside time to evaluate the various facets of her life.

Maria's and Pamela's stories highlight the fourth rule of spiritual living by reason:

Avoid shallow and transient pleasures. Keep your life simple. Seek calming pleasures that contribute to peace of mind. True pleasure is disciplined and restrained.

In its many shapes and forms, pleasure is what every human being is after. It is the chief good of life. Yet not all pleasures are alike. Some pleasures are kinetic—shallow and transient, fading away as soon as the acts that created them end. Often they are succeeded by a feeling of emptiness and psychological pain and suffering. Other pleasures are *catastematic*—deep and prolonged, continuing even after the acts that created them end; it is these pleasures that secure the well-lived life. That's the message of the Epicurean philosophers, who have been maligned and misunderstood for centuries, particularly in the modern era where their theories of the good life have been confused with doctrines advocating gross hedonism.

By way of illustration, people who have wrongly dedicated themselves to kinetic pleasures, as Maria did, end up on a treadmill, constantly in need of a new supply of pleasurable stimuli in order to sustain an acceptable existence. Flash-in-the-pan enjoyments, like fine dining, all-night entertainment, and engagement in meaningless sexual activity, are pleasurable only as long as they last. Once completed, these kinetic pleasures immediately cease to supply delight, and may even produce long-term pain and suffering for the agent.

Despite their reputation, the Epicureans constantly warned of the negative consequences associated with the gratification of excessive and unnatural desires. The glutton who consumes food in violation of reasonable limits experiences discomfort and illness, just as the sex addict who recklessly engages in sexual activity risks sexually transmitted diseases and unwanted pregnancy. The greedy business executives who want it all end up losing it all, as do corrupt government officials who use their positions to enrich themselves rather than serve the public. True pleasure requires limits and restraints, in the absence of which even natural pleasures can become a source of pain, suffering, and sorrow. Indulgence of legitimate bodily and psychological needs involves naturally pleasure-granting activities, but they must be guided by considerations of constraint and consequence.

Learning to steer clear of kinetic pleasures and toward *catastematic* pleasures isn't a single-session lesson, but a daily discipline leading to what Epicureans called *ataraxia*, or peace of mind, the highest pleasure that can be achieved, a state of mental equilibrium that precludes the inner turmoil suggested by the modern term *stress*. Anyone who has spent a sleepless night worrying about the complexities of daily life should understand the importance of attaining such a state of mental and emotional calm.

To find the path to *ataraxia,* wise people conduct an inventory of their priorities, attachments, values, and activities for the purpose of uncomplicating their lives.

People involved in a high-pressure job with long hours and enormous pressures must ask whether the emotional and psychological anxieties routinely experienced are worth the financial rewards. At some point, people interested in true quality of life must ask, “Is this really worth it? Isn’t there more to life than this stress-driven rat-race?” Only when individuals begin to reflect along these lines can they start the process of attaining *ataraxia*. Once achieved, the spiritual benefits of such a life far outweigh the anxiety-provoking compensations of wealth and status. As the modern medical community continues to warn, stress kills—it can contribute directly to high blood pressure, stroke, and heart disease. *Ataraxia* is the ancient world’s equivalent to biofeedback, and as a life strategy it may be more relevant today than ever before.

THE MEDITATION GRID

≈ *Don't gratify shallow, transient, and unnatural pleasures and desires.*

≈ *Seek stable, calming pleasures that contribute to peace of mind.*

≈ *Keep your life simple.*

≈ *Seek* ataraxia, *the mental equilibrium that keeps you mentally and emotionally calm.*

≈ *When getting yourself into a stress situation, ask yourself: "Is this really worth it? Isn't there more to life than this stress-driven treadmill?"*

Rule 5

Master Yourself

No person is free who is not master of himself.

—Epictetus

Rule 5

Master Yourself

John was a successful car mechanic. He was a master in his field. He could perform magic on car engines, identifying and correcting even the most difficult problems. He was also a good family man, raising three children and putting them through school, and a good citizen, casting his vote in local and national elections. But he wasn't master of himself, of the inner desires that shaped his lifestyle. He was a heavy smoker and drinker, and he constantly craved junk food. Worse, he never tried to honestly assess his inner desires. Instead, he deceived himself by rationalizing his misguided desires with all kinds of spurious arguments, like "people don't die from smoking, drinking, and eating; they die from the stress and anxieties created by the restrictions doctors impose on them." As it turned out, they do! John passed away in his late forties from a massive heart attack.

John's story is neither new nor unique. It highlights people's failure to master themselves, underlining the fifth rule of spiritual living by reason:

> RESIST ANY EXTERNAL FORCE THAT MIGHT DELIMIT THOUGHT AND ACTION; STOP DECEIVING YOURSELF, BELIEVING ONLY WHAT IS PERSONALLY USEFUL AND CONVENIENT; COMPLETE LIBERTY NECESSITATES A STRUGGLE WITHIN, A BATTLE TO SUBDUE NEGATIVE PSYCHOLOGICAL AND SPIRITUAL FORCES THAT PRECLUDE A HEALTHY EXISTENCE; SELF-MASTERY REQUIRES RUTHLESS CANDOR.

One of the more concrete ties between ancient and modern times is the idea that personal freedom is a highly desirable state and one of life's great blessings. Today, freedom tends to be associated, above all, with political liberty. Therefore, freedom is often perceived as a reward for political struggle, measured in terms of one's ability to exercise individual "rights." This is especially the case in true democratic societies, like the United States and the European Union, where individual freedoms and rights are warranted by law and people consider themselves the masters of their own lives.

Yet individuals who are fully protected under a system of political rights and enjoy immunity from external oppression may not be fully protected from negative physiological and spiritual forces. Democratic constitutions and laws allocate citizens' freedoms and protect them from oppression, but they do not reach far enough to assure the more comprehensive freedom implied by Epictetus's term *self-mastery.*

Long before Sigmund Freud and the advent of modern psychology, the ancients argued that the acquisition of genuine freedom involved a dual battle. First, a battle without, against any external force that might delimit thought and action. Second, a battle within, a struggle to subdue psychological and spiritual forces that preclude a healthy self-reliance. The ancient wisdom clearly recognized that humankind has an infinite capacity for self-deception, to believe what is personally useful and convenient at the expense of truth and reality, all with catastrophic consequences. Individual investors often deceive themselves by holding on to shady stocks, believing what they want to believe. They often end up blaming stock analysts and stockbrokers when the truth of the matter is they are the ones who eventually made the decision to buy the stocks in the first place. Students also deceive themselves into believing that they can pass a course without studying, and end up blaming their professors for their eventual failure. Patients also deceive themselves that they can be cured with convenient "alternative medicines," which do not involve the restrictive lifestyle of conventional methods.

Self-mastery isn't a divine endowment people receive at birth, but a daily struggle, an inner war, a combat between rational and irrational elements, which is far more difficult and intimidating than any struggle against external opponents. Winning this war takes a ruthless honesty and a capacity to critically assess the choices, values, and lifestyle by which we choose to live: it requires that we stop blaming others for our shortcomings or wasting time manufacturing excuses. In the process of reconstructing themselves self-mastered people proceed without pity or leniency: they candidly assess their weaknesses, particularly the bad habits that undermine their well-being.

Most fundamentally, self-mastery requires the full understanding of who we are, and an accurate and unambiguous self-image that nourishes, informs, and updates everything we do. Self-mastery requires an inner direction and self-determination in accordance with standards and principles arrived at through the crucible of critical self-examination. Self-mastered people are self-assured without being self-satisfied, quietly confident without being vain or proud. In short, the self-mastered individual represents the integrated personality, a person operating at the highest level of human functioning deemed "free" because the highest liberty is an understanding of self devoid of illusion.

The Meditation Grid

≈ *Resist any external force that might distort your thoughts and actions.*

≈ *Avoid convenient and self-justifying rationalizations.*

≈ *Complete liberty necessitates a struggle within, a battle to subdue psychological and spiritual forces that preclude a healthy self-reliance.*

≈ *Be ruthlessly honest with yourself; always critically assess your motives.*

≈ *Don't blame others for your shortcomings.*

≈ *The highest liberty is an understanding of self devoid of illusion.*

RULE 6

AVOID EXCESS

Nothing in excess.
—Solon

Rule 6

Avoid Excess

In almost every aspect of her life, Marisa has always been a woman of excesses. Some days she carefully watches her diet, almost starving herself. Other days, she eats everything she finds in front of her. Some weekends, she will go out all night long. Other weekends, she will stay home lying on the couch, watching soap operas. Sometimes, she goes on spending sprees, taking on unmanageable credit card debt for things she has no use for. Other times, she refuses to buy essentials like coffee, milk, and bread.

Marisa typifies people who let themselves live in a world of excess, highlighting the sixth rule of spiritual living by reason:

LIVE A LIFE OF HARMONY AND BALANCE. AVOID EXCESSES. STEER BETWEEN EXTREMES. EVEN GOOD THINGS, PURSUED OR ATTAINED WITHOUT MODERATION, CAN BECOME A SOURCE OF MISERY AND SUFFERING.

This rule is echoed in the writings of ancient Greek thinkers who viewed moderation as nothing less than a solution to life's riddle. The idea of avoiding the many opportunities for excess was a prime ingredient in a life properly lived, as summarized in Solon's prescription "nothing in excess" (sixth century BCE). The Greeks fully grasped the high costs of passionate excess. They correctly understood that when people violate the limits of a reasonable mean, they pay penalties ranging from countervailing frustrations to utter catastrophe. It is for this reason that they prized ideals such as measure, balance, harmony, and proportion as much as they did, the parameters within which productive living can proceed. If, however, excess is allowed to destroy harmony and balance, then a life worth living becomes impossible to obtain.

These postulates are as urgent and compelling today as they ever have been—perhaps more so. Unlike our ancient counterparts, we live in times that are fraught with opportunity for excess and waste—indeed, our society encourages and promotes disproportion of every kind, in eating, in dressing, in home life, in driving, and in entertainment. We often end up buying food we never eat, clothes we never wear, and cars we rarely drive.

In comparative terms, life in antiquity was simple. Levels of technological and material development were positively primitive by modern standards. Accordingly, the opportunities for distraction and allurement were correspondingly less. In other words, there were simply fewer chances to live excessively two thousand years ago than there are today. Modern culture has not only produced a spate of seductions, it has also developed the means to promote and persuade people to live at an indulgent extreme. In particular, commercial advertising has fashioned a view of human realization that insists life must be "lived to the max"; that is, more food, more money, more luxury, more power. The message of modern culture is clear, "limits are for losers," with the result that those who consciously attempt to live lives guided by proportion and harmony are seen as naively out of step with the "good" life.

What needs to be considered here are the deleterious effects of a culture dedicated to excess. In a recent television broadcast extolling the lifestyle of the rich and famous, a pair of diamond-encrusted basketball sneakers were displayed costing $50,000. The same show also presented a wristwatch worth $1 million and a home in South Florida worth $30 million. We should all be very clear about what these items represent—they are not simply a violation of the mean, they are a tasteless mockery of anything suggestive of limit. Commodities such as these are a clear indication of a social pathology reflecting distorted values. Unfortunately, what these big-ticket consumers typically discover at some point later in their lives is that distorted values eventually produce distorted lives. The lesson learned from the life of glitter is that disproportion is the thief of real happiness. The fancy car does not immunize against divorce; the cigarette boat is no protection against drug addiction; and the mansion in Hollywood doesn't keep you off the therapist's couch.

To live a life of balance and moderation is not to live life ascetically. A monastic existence, with its many prohibitions and denials, itself constitutes a kind of violation of the mean. No, the ancients were not prescribing a diet of wild honey and locusts. Rather, they advocated a carefully crafted life strategically situated between extremes. Food is a good and necessary aspect of life, but gluttony and starvation are distortions. Material prosperity is a desirable and essential feature of a good life, but neither obscene wealth nor abject poverty is productive of human felicity. Above all, the message of Solon involves the idea that even good things, pursued or attained immoderately, can become a source of misery. The key is to recognize that there are circumstances when less is more. This is a particularly difficult lesson for us to accept in the modern era given the remarkable abundance with which we are surrounded. Nevertheless, if our lives lack the equilibrium implied by the phrase "nothing in excess," we will never experience the physical, mental, and spiritual contentment requisite for a life worth living. To live in balance is therefore a rule for life we can ill afford to ignore.

The Meditation Grid

≈ ***Seek harmony, balance, and proportion.***

≈ ***Preserve the mean. Avoid extremes.***

≈ ***Even good things, pursued or attained immoderately, can become a source of misery.***

≈ ***Disproportion is the thief of real happiness.***

≈ ***In some circumstances, less is actually more.***

Rule 7

Be a Responsible Human Being

Reproach yourself for the things you do wrong.
—Pythagoras

Rule 7

Be a Responsible Human Being

Tracy has rarely assumed responsibility for her actions, constantly blaming others for her errors and shortcomings. When at school, she blamed her teachers for her bad grades, her fellow students for not helping her with homework, and her parents for not being attuned to her personal problems. But she never blamed herself for having her priorities wrong, for spending hours in front of the television set watching one sitcom after another rather than studying for school, and for cutting classes to spend time in the nearby cafes. When at work, she blamed her boss for giving her biased and unfair reviews rather than herself for being late to work, for refusing to get along with her co-workers, and for failing to accomplish the work assigned to her. When dating someone, Tracy wasn't honest with herself, denying responsibility for what went wrong in the relationship. In the end, Tracy's lack of responsibility and honesty crippled every opportunity, every relationship, and every prospect for a meaningful life.

Tracy's story typifies and underscores the seventh rule of spiritual living by reason:

Reproach yourself with honesty and thoroughness for wrongdoing; maintain a kind of spiritual hygiene; stop the blame-shifting for your errors and shortcomings. Be honest with yourself and be prepared to assume responsibility and to accept consequences.

This rule comes from Pythagoras, the famous mathematician and mystic, and has special relevance for all of us because of the common human tendency to reject responsibility for wrongdoing. Very few individuals are willing to hold themselves accountable for the errors and mishaps that inevitably occur in life. Instead, they tend to foist these situations off on others, complaining of circumstances "beyond their control." There are, of course, situations that occasionally sweep us along, against which we have little or no recourse. But far more typically, we find ourselves in dilemmas of our own creation—dilemmas for which we refuse to be held accountable. How many times does the average person say something like, "It really wasn't my fault. If only John or Mary had acted differently, then I would not have responded as I did." Cop-outs like these are the standard reaction for most people. They reflect an infinite human capacity for rationalization, finger-pointing, and denial of responsibility. Unfortunately, this penchant for excuses and self-exemption has negative consequences. People who feed themselves a steady diet of exonerating fiction are in danger of living life in bad faith—more, they risk corrupting their very essence as human beings.

Pythagoras is best known for the theorem that bears his name and least known for a soul doctrine relating directly to human character. He believed the soul was the highest and best part of a human being and that the top priority in life was the proper care and treatment of our spiritual portion. It was for this reason that Pythagoras imposed a strict code of conduct upon his followers, which included a demand for exemplary personal conduct. Reproaching oneself honestly and thoroughly for wrong-doing was apparently part of the personal discipline he prescribed for his disciples. In doing so, Pythagoras believed a person was best able to maintain a kind of spiritual hygiene. Conversely, those who consistently engaged in blame-shifting, those who routinely denied their role in errors and misdeeds, were risking the health of their souls. Sadly, the human ability to "manufacture" truth may be unlimited, but there is one form of falsehood that is particularly lethal to human happiness—the self-deceiving lie. It is the "grand" dishonesty that distorts and cripples every opportunity, every relationship, and every prospect for a meaningful life. The antidote for this sickness is honest and detailed self-incrimination, a true willingness to candidly confess responsibility and not assign to others blame best assigned to oneself.

Also implicit in Pythagoras's observation is the notion of consequence. A full and forthright acceptance of responsibility must also include a corresponding willingness to accept consequences. In the absence of such willingness, all gestures of self-reproach become meaningless. We see many examples of this in contemporary society. The politicians, the corporate executives, and the attorneys who stand before the cameras and dramatically declare their willingness to accept "full responsibility." But in the end, there is no resignation, no prosecution, no real consequence of any kind. Public displays such as these are more theater than they are genuine self-indictment and as a result they constitute a kind of double dishonesty. They reflect neither a true acceptance of responsibility nor an honest interest in personal assessment. Such individuals forfeit the benefit of Pythagoras's insight, namely, that honesty with self is one of life's great imperatives, without which healthy, mature personhood is unattainable.

The Meditation Grid

≈ *The "grand" dishonesty—the self-deceiving lie—is lethal to human happiness. It distorts and cripples every opportunity, every relationship, and every prospect for a meaningful life.*

≈ *Reproach yourself honestly and thoroughly for wrongdoing; maintain a proper spiritual hygiene; stop the blame-shifting for your errors and shortcomings.*

≈ *Be prepared to candidly confess responsibility and not assign to others a blame best assigned to yourself, and be willing to accept consequences.*

Rule 8

Don't Be a Prosperous Fool

A prosperous fool is a grievous burden.
—Aeschylus

Rule 8

Don't Be a Prosperous Fool

John has always been obsessed with wealth accumulation. At the age of twenty-one, he quit college to join a major firm as financial advisor. By the age of twenty-five, he was earning a six-figure income, living in a comfortable house and owning a portfolio of stocks worth close to $1 million. By the age of thirty-five, John extended his asset holdings to real estate, collectibles, speedboats, and designer watches, which he never missed the chance to display and brag about in his investment seminars. "Life is about wealth accumulation," he used to say with arrogance to young recruits. "Money can buy you everything, all the trophies in the world. It certainly did that for me."

In amassing his wealth, John was ruthless and at times reckless, compromising his own integrity, destroying meaningful human relationships, and creating a life devoid of meaning and purpose. He never hesitated to take advantage of everyone who came his way, including his parents, mortgaging their prime residence to invest in financial markets; his uncle with disabilities, churning his accident settlement money to earn commissions; and his retired neighbor, selling him unsuitable financial products to maximize his own rather than his client's returns. He never took someone out to lunch unless he expected something out of it. He never contemplated marriage and family, because he considered them a distraction from making money. He spared no time for anything but the cultivation of his portfolio.

Now in his early sixties, John lives alone in an empty mansion without family, without friends, and without neighbors. He has finally begun to understand that wealth alone is not the key to happiness.

John's story is neither new nor unique. History is full of examples of people who became rich by destroying their relations and serving as a bad model for those who followed them. Two such examples are the idols of the American Gilded Age, Andrew Carnegie and John Rockefeller, who amassed their fortunes by exploitation and oppressing their workers and partners.

John's life and the early lives of Andrew Carnegie and John Rockefeller underline and highlight the eighth rule of spiritual living by reason:

Prosperity, in and of itself, is not a cure-all against an ill-led life, and may be a source of dangerous foolishness. Money is a necessary but not a sufficient component for the good life, for happiness and wisdom.

Prosperity has different meanings to different people. For some, prosperity is about the accumulation of wealth in the form of money, real estate, and equities. For others, prosperity is about the accumulation of power and the achievement of status that comes with appointment to business or government positions. In either case, prosperity requires wisdom—the rational use of one's resources and energies. In the absence of such wisdom, Aeschylus was correct to speak of prosperous fools.

All too often people assume that by merely acquiring wealth, all will fall into place, ensuring them a happy and fulfilled existence. While achieving financial security is a necessary step in the quest for happiness and a good life, it isn't sufficient. People who acquire wealth but in the process compromise their own integrity destroy meaningful human relationships and create a life devoid of meaning and purpose, as John, Andrew Carnegie, and John Rockefeller did. In the end what have they really gained?

Individuals who associate prosperity with a happy and meaningful life truly are fools, prosperous though they may be, because they have completely misunderstood the hierarchy of values that necessarily governs a properly lived life. Fools fail to understand that money is a device, a tool, a practical asset whose worth lies in its capacity to attain objects of intrinsic value. Money, in other words, is a means to higher and more important ends. It is not an end in itself. Failure to grasp this point has produced immeasurable chaos and misery. And it is in this sense that Aeschylus was entirely correct: prosperous fools are a burden and, first and foremost, they are burdens to themselves because by not recognizing the purely instrumental nature of wealth they condemn themselves to lives devoid of merit and substance.

Aeschylus's reference to "burden" does not end with the self-inflicted wounds of the prosperous fool, however. Fools possessing significant financial resources also have a capacity to promote and disseminate their unsound perspectives throughout society. This is particularly the case in times such as ours where the impact of mass media has become inescapable. Television, movies, and print images too often advance the lifestyle of these individuals as an ideal worthy of emulation. As a result, the misguided perspectives of the wealthy fool have an opportunity to serve as a kind of general cultural standard and in doing so become a "grievous burden" for an entire society. What is not typically reported amid the gaiety and glitter is the wreckage associated with the joining of prosperity and foolishness—the drug use, the failed marriages, the continuous sense of dissatisfaction with life.

In short, Aeschylus's maxim carries three clear messages for people who think that prosperity solves all problems and assures a good and meaningful life. The first message is that wealth offers no immunity against error and stupidity. People who display considerable skill and insight in amassing a fortune may be fundamentally ignorant of life's most important lessons. The second message is that great care should be exercised in designating cultural models. Wealth per se is not a guarantee of happiness, to say nothing of wisdom. Accordingly, we must guard against prosperous fools becoming cultural icons. Failure here means the well-off fools are no longer simply a burden to themselves but become generalized burdens to the entire culture. The third message is that each of us has an obligation to ourselves and to our communities not to be fools. This is, perhaps, the greatest of all wisdoms the Greeks have to offer the modern world. We are rational animals and as such the joy we seek can never be secured in the absence of intelligence. No amount of money, power, or privilege can deliver us from the shortcomings of a fool's existence.

The Meditation Grid

≈ ***Wealth per se is no guarantee for happiness and wisdom.***

≈ ***Wealth offers no immunity against error and stupidity.***

≈ ***Prosperity must be ruled by wisdom.***

≈ ***No amount of money, power, or privilege can deliver us from the shortcomings of a fool's existence.***

Rule 9

Don't Do Evil to Others

The man who does evil to others does evil to himself.

—Hesiod

Rule 9

Don't Do Evil to Others

Patrick has always been someone who likes to plot and scheme, to manipulate people and get them into trouble. When in school, he used to set up fellow students against the teacher by giving them the wrong homework assignment or the wrong answers, and he would set one student against another by spreading rumors and false allegations. When he got his first job as a sales consultant in a department store, he upped the stakes. He spread rumors against his co-workers and his boss. Sometimes, his motive was a hefty bonus or a fast-track promotion. At other times, his motive was just to make others look bad and himself good. In either case, wrongdoing to others became a habit that corrupted his personality and poisoned his relations, turning him into a bitter, grudging, joyless, and neurotic person, living in constant fear that others would do to him what he had done to them.

Patrick's story exemplifies the ninth rule of spiritual living by reason:

EVILDOING IS A DANGEROUS HABIT, A KIND OF REFLEX TOO QUICKLY RESORTED TO AND TOO EASILY JUSTIFIED THAT HAS A LASTING AND DAMAGING EFFECT UPON THE QUEST FOR THE GOOD LIFE. HARMING OTHERS CLAIMS TWO VICTIMS—THE VICTIM, THE RECEIVER OF HARM, AND THE VICTIMIZER, THE ONE WHO DOES HARM. OVER TIME, EVILDOING PROLIFERATES AND FESTERS UNTIL IT CORRUPTS THE ENTIRE PERSONALITY, RESULTING IN A PERSON RIFE WITH EMOTIONAL AND PSYCHOLOGICAL DISORDERS.

Contemporary society is filled with mixed messages when it comes to the treatment of our fellow human beings. The message of the Judeo-Christian religious heritage, for instance, is that doing evil to others is a sin; it extols the virtues of mercy, forgiveness, charity, love, and pacifism. Yet, as we all know, in practice these inspiring ideals tend to be in short supply. Modern society is a competitive, hard-bitten environment strongly inclined to advocate self-advantage at the expense of the "other." Under these conditions, it is not surprising that people are often prepared to harm their fellow human beings. These activities are frequently justified by invoking premises such as "payback," "leveling scores," or "doing unto others before they can do unto you." Implicit in all of these phrases is the notion that malice toward others can be justified on a reciprocal basis or as a preemptive gesture in advance of anticipated injury. What is not considered here is the effects these attempts to render evil have upon the person engaging in such endeavors. Our culture has naively assumed that "getting even" is an acceptable response to wrongdoing—that one bad turn deserves another. What we fail to understand is the psychological, emotional, and spiritual impact victimizing others has upon the victimizer.

Hesiod was an ancient Greek poet who opposed evildoing from a rationalistic perspective. He recognized two crucially important points about the effects of evildoing on the wrongdoer. First, evildoing can easily become a habit, a kind of reflex too quickly resorted to and too easily justified. Second, individuals who develop a habit of hurting others suffer spiritual impoverishment; they are diminished as human beings and are correspondingly debilitated in the quest for the good life. This means that evildoing has a rebounding effect. When someone harms another person, there are two victims—the receiver of harm and the one who does harm. It is this consequence of evildoing most people today find difficult to believe or accept, namely, that damaging others constitutes a kind of self-inflicted spiritual wound that eventually turns evildoers into bitter, grudging, and joyless people. Evildoers also suffer a loss of opportunity with regard to breathing the rarefied air of the "high road"—a powerful source of spiritual enhancement.

Conversely, those who consistently refrain from injuring others, even when doing so might be warranted by conventional standards, are often rewarded by a sense of quiet contentment and inner peace. Unlike those who allow evildoing to infect their spirit, people who remain superior to these base instincts often experience a profound sense of self-satisfaction stemming from their uncommon discipline and restraint. They correctly come to see themselves as operating at a higher spiritual level as a result of having renounced things like vindictiveness and revenge. Rather than expend energy on plots and intrigues, people who avoid harming others have an opportunity to concentrate their efforts on constructive activities productive of tranquility and happiness. Their lives are richer and more fulfilled because they refuse to compromise their dignity and worth by engaging in actions that might demean their stature as properly functioning human beings.

It should be noted that the ancient Greeks were not pacifists in these matters. Hesiod is not proposing we should "turn the other cheek," and he would never have suggested people should refrain from defending themselves against the evil intentions of enemies. His true message is simply this: human beings must not only avoid staining their souls with evil; they should also do everything in their power to experience the exhilaration of being decent human beings.

The Meditation Grid

≈ ***Don't stain your soul with evil.***

≈ ***Evildoing is a dangerous habit; it harms both the victim and the victimizer.***

≈ ***Victimizers become bitter, grudging, joyless, and neurotic persons.***

≈ ***Experience the exhilaration of being a decent human being.***

≈ ***Concentrate your efforts on constructive activities that yield tranquility and happiness.***

Rule 10

Kindness toward Others Tends to Be Rewarded

No act of kindness is ever wasted.

—Aesop

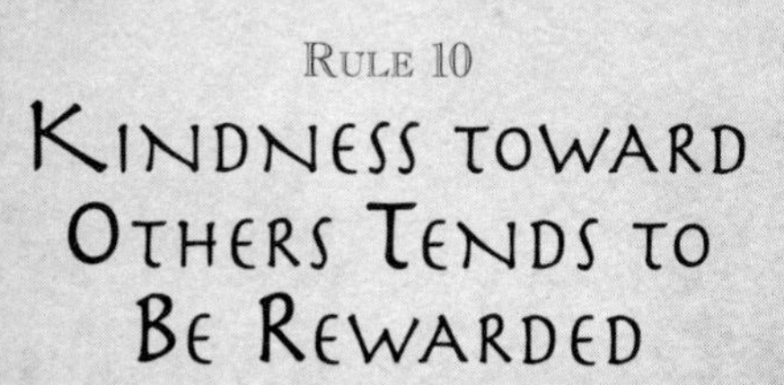

Rule 10

Kindness toward Others Tends to Be Rewarded

Bob has always been kind to people. In childhood, Bob was kind to his younger siblings, always looking after them, always advising them. In his school years, Bob assisted his fellow students with homework assignments, lent them lunch money, and tried to build bridges among those who fought with each other. Eventually, by being kind to others, Bob developed a warm and pleasant personality that attracted and magnetized people around him, helping him expand his own horizons, emotionally and spiritually.

Bob's story highlights the tenth rule of spiritual living by reason:

Kindness to others is a good habit that has a lasting effect that supports and reinforces the quest for the good life. Helping others bestows a sense of satisfaction that has two beneficiaries—the beneficiary, the receiver of the help, and the benefactor, the one who provides the help. Over time people who do good deeds develop a friendly and joyful personality that attracts and magnetizes those they associate with and brings kindness their way.

Many of the world's great religions speak of an obligation to extend kindness to others. But these deeds are often advocated as an investment toward future salvation—as the admission ticket to paradise. That's not the case for the ancient Greeks, however, who saw kindness through the lens of reason, emphasizing the positive effects acts of kindness have not just on the receiver of kindness but on the giver of kindness as well, not for the salvation of the soul in the afterlife but in this life. Simply put, kindness tends to return to those who do kind deeds, as Aesop demonstrated in his colorful fable of a little mouse cutting the net to free the big lion. Aesop lived in the sixth century BCE and acquired a great reputation in antiquity for the instruction he offered in his delightful tales. Despite the passage of many centuries, Aesop's counsels have stood the test of time because in truth, they are timeless observations on the human condition, as relevant and meaningful today as they were more than two thousand years ago.

As it happens, the ancient Greeks were not as "idealistic" as they are sometimes portrayed as being. Even the great philosophers and poets among them were strongly inclined toward utility in many of their teachings—including the notion of good deeds. The idea of an act of kindness as an end in itself or as a matter of personal duty was simply not part of their moral horizon. At the same time, however, their sense of utility in such matters was not crass or tactless. For Aesop an act of kindness is not a calculation; it is not a conscious investment made in the hope of attaining a dividend. What he suggests, instead, is that beneficence tends to return to those who do good deeds—a kind of karmic recompense. And so in Aesop's fable, when the lion is hopelessly ensnared in a net, it is the lowly mouse the lion once spared that nibbles through the ropes and sets him free—a spontaneous good deed reciprocated under circumstances no one could have anticipated.

In our own day, Aesop's premise that no kindness is wasted carries two strong messages for modern relationships that tend to encourage self-indulgence and the advancement of individual ego. The first message is that we are social creatures, that we need the "other" in order to fulfill our own lives. This message is often lost when so much time and energy are invested in advancing one's own causes, leaving little opportunity to reach out to others. At least part of the neurotic behavior we see in modern society—the alienation, the substance abuse, the depression—is undoubtedly related to the absence of meaningful social relationships. For Aesop, human benevolence can be seen as a facilitating feature in establishing social bonds. In the absence of a kind gesture, barriers remain and people are unwilling to trust or commit. But when one human being takes a chance and offers the "other" a genuine expression of kindness—something not owed, but gratuitously extended—then the entire social dynamic is altered. Now the path is clear for real connection, for the establishment of what has been called the "I-thou" relationship. These relationships, it should be noted, are of a kind that tends to matter most in life.

The second message is that kindness has a positive effect on a benefactor. A strong case can be made for the idea that generosity toward others contributes to the human development of the one extending the act of kindness. In helping others we expand our own horizons, emotionally and spiritually. We grow as human beings, acquiring a new understanding of ourselves and our attachments to others. Above all, rendering a kindness to another human being can bestow a profound sense of satisfaction. Doers of generous deeds, those who do not ask "what's in it for me?" but simply extend themselves gratuitously experience a sense of inner contentment that elevates and ennobles. Such individuals are entitled to view themselves positively because they are more complete in their personhood than others.

In sum, acts of kindness create real opportunity for relationships by breaking down walls that isolate and divide. In terms of personal development, generosity toward others may have a self-actualizing effect by which the benefactor moves to a higher level of spiritual fulfillment and contentment. In addition, it may be hoped that "what goes around, comes around"; that men and women of genial heart create circumstances whereby they become the recipients of similar kindnesses—as the lion was repaid by the mouse.

The Meditation Grid

≈ *Be generous to others.*

≈ *Generosity creates real opportunities for lowering the walls that isolate and divide us.*

≈ *Kindness bestows a profound sense of satisfaction.*

≈ *A true act of kindness is not a calculation; it is not a conscious investment made in the hope of attaining a dividend.*

≈ *Beneficence tends to return to those who do good deeds.*

Epilogue

Spiritual living is not an exclusive preserve of religious teaching. There are alternative paths to spiritual contentment, one of which involves the examined life afforded by reason. Among reason's many blessings are a capacity to examine life; to understand what we can and what we cannot control in life; to discriminate between false and true pleasures; to identify true friendships; to attain a properly balanced existence—all of which can contribute to a meaningful spirituality, such as that outlined by the wisdom of the ancient Greek sages.

1. **Examine life.** Engage life with a vengeance; always search for new opportunities to expand your mental and spiritual horizons.

2. **Worry only about the things you can control.** Worry about the things that can be influenced and changed by your actions, not about things beyond your control,

the things that cannot be influenced and changed by your actions.

3. **TREASURE FRIENDSHIP.** Friendship is a reciprocal attachment that fills the need for affiliation. Friendship cannot be acquired in the marketplace, but must be nurtured and treasured in relations imbued by trust and immersed in amity.

4. **EXPERIENCE TRUE PLEASURE.** Avoid shallow and transient indulgences. Keep your life simple. Seek calming experiences that contribute to peace of mind. True pleasures contain natural limits.

5. **MASTER YOURSELF.** Resist any external force that might delimit thought and action; stop deceiving yourself, believing only what is personally useful and convenient. Complete liberty necessitates a struggle within, a battle to subdue psychological and spiritual forces that preclude a healthy self-reliance. Be ruthlessly honest with yourself.

6. **AVOID EXCESS.** Live a life of harmony and balance. Avoid excesses. Steer between extremes. Even good things, pursued

or attained without moderation, can become a source of misery and suffering.

7. **Be a responsible human being.** Reproach yourself with honesty and thoroughness for wrongdoing; maintain spiritual hygiene; stop the blame-shifting for your errors and shortcomings. The "grand" dishonesty—the self-deceiving lie—is lethal to your happiness. It distorts and cripples every opportunity, every relationship, and every prospect for a meaningful life. Be aggressively self-indicting; be prepared to candidly confess responsibility; and be willing to accept consequences.

8. **Don't be a prosperous fool.** Prosperity, of and in itself, is not cure-all against an ill-led life and may be a source of dangerous folly. Money is a necessary but not a sufficient component of the good life.

9. **Don't do evil to others.** Evildoing is a dangerous habit, a kind of reflex too quickly resorted to and too easily justified that has a detrimental effect that undermines

the quest for the good life. Harming others claims two victims—the victim, the receiver of harm, and the victimizer, the one who does harm. Over time wounds such as these expand and fester until they corrupt the entire personality, resulting in a person who is bitter, grudging, joyless, and neurotic.

10. KINDNESS TOWARD OTHERS TENDS TO BE REWARDED. Kindness to others is a good habit that has a lasting and positive effect that supports and reinforces the quest for the good life. Helping others bestows a sense of satisfaction that has two beneficiaries—the beneficiary, the receiver of the help, and the benefactor, the one who provides the help. Over time people who do good deeds develop a friendly and joyful personality that attracts and engages other human beings.

About the Authors

Michael A. Soupios is a professor at Long Island University's C. W. Post Campus, where he has taught for more than thirty years, receiving several teaching awards. Professor Soupios holds eight graduate degrees, including four earned doctorates. His areas of expertise include philosophy, history, classics, political science, and religion. The author of numerous articles and papers on a variety of classical subjects, Professor Soupios has recently published a full-length study on the cultural history of Ancient Greece entitled *The Song of Hellas* (2004). Professor Soupios frequently conducts workshops and seminars in spiritual living. He resides in East Northport, New York, with his wife and three children.

Panos Mourdoukoutas is a professor at Long Island's C. W. Post Campus, where he has taught for twenty-five years. Professor Mourdoukoutas has traveled extensively throughout the world, lecturing on business strategy and leadership at a number of universities, businesses, and community organizations. He is the author of several articles published in professional journals and magazines, including the *New York Times, Japan Times, Barron's*, and *Edge Singapore*. He has also published several books, including *New Emerging Japanese Economy: Opportunity and Strategy for World Business* (Thompson/South-Western, 2005) and *Business Strategy in a Semiglobal Economy* (Sharpe, 2006). In 2001, he received the Emerald Literati Club's Highly Commended Award for Excellence.

Hampton Roads Publishing Company

. . . for the evolving human spirit